THE
FISHING
INDUSTRY

BY NANCY WARREN FERRELL

FRANKLIN WATTS
New York ▪ London ▪ Toronto ▪ Sydney
A FIRST BOOK ▪ 1984

TO RUSTY AND
TO THE FAMILY

Cover photograph courtesy of Shostal

Photographs courtesy of:
U.S. National Marine Fisheries Service, Alaska:
pp. 6, 26, 43, 45;
Alaska Department of Fish and Game:
pp. 15, 20, 29, 31, 47;
Alaska Seafood Marketing Institute: p. 37.

Map and illustrations by Vantage Art

Library of Congress Cataloging in Publication Data

Ferrell, Nancy Warren.
The fishing industry.

(A First book)
Bibliography: p.
Includes index.
Summary: An introduction to fishing as an industry,
describing how fish are caught, problems of
fishermen, and the future of the fishing industry.
1. Fish trade—United States—Juvenile literature.
2. Fishermen—United States—Juvenile literature.
3. Seafood—United States—Juvenile literature.
4. Fishing—United States—Juvenile literature.
5. Fishes—United States—Juvenile literature.
[1. Fishing. 2. Fish trade] I. Title.
HD9455.F47 1984   338.3'7270973   84-5258
ISBN 0-531-04823-3

CONTENTS

Grateful acknowledgment is made to
Dr. William Smoker, retired director of the
National Marine Fisheries Service's Laboratory,
Auke Bay, Alaska, for his kindness in checking
the manuscript of this work for fishing accuracy.
I also wish to thank
fisherman Ted Merrell; and the staffs of
the National Marine Fisheries Service, Juneau, Alaska;
the Alaska Department of Fish and Game;
the Alaska Department of Labor;
the Alaska Seafood Marketing Institute;
the Alaska Department of Environmental Conservation
for their generous help in supplying information
and/or illustrative material for this book.

N.W.F.

1

FISH AND THEIR WORLD

Rick Sorenson undid the bowline from the dock and flipped it onto the deck of the *Cora Jean.* He signaled to his father on the **bridge,** took a few strides, and hiked himself over the rail onto the stern. The deck hummed from the diesel beneath his feet. A light mist sprayed his face.

He stood watching the line of boats as the *Cora Jean* backed from the stall, drifted to **starboard,** slowed, and then chugged forward, heading out of the harbor at Juneau, Alaska. Once past the breakers, the 48-footer (11.63 m) cut through the rolling swell.

It would be a long run to Taku for **gill-net** fishing, but Rick did not mind. He liked working with his dad, earning money, and living the life of a fisherman. There was no better summer job.

Rick glanced up.

If the weather holds, he thought, we'll make Salisbury Point before noon.

In spite of the July morning, a chill wind whipped across the water. Rick hitched his jacket collar close around his neck, and went inside.

FISHING FROM ANCIENT TIMES

Rick had never thought about the science of commercial fishing. He had grown up in the industry, as had his father and his father's father. His ancestors fished the fjords of Norway for hundreds of years before coming to America. However, fishing was important long before Rick's ancestors settled in Scandinavia.

Indians fished on the North American continent many years before the United States became a country. Even back in earliest cave-dweller times, humans fished, using birds' beaks for hooks and plant stalks for lines. Though fish might have been difficult to catch due to lack of efficient gear, shellfish were picked up easily. Mounds of castoff shells from ancient days have been found in China, Denmark, Brazil, and the United States.

Eventually, people settled near streams and rivers to have a means of easy travel, and for a food supply. The need for more food—more and bigger fish—encouraged fishermen to build larger boats. It further forced them to develop better methods and gear, and to travel ever farther away from shore. People grouped together on ships to share the work. With bigger catches, they could sell the fish they did not need for their own needs. As early as 4,000 years ago, pictures carved in stone told of fish caught by hand nets and sold from the Nile River in Egypt. Thus commercial fisheries were born and developed through the centuries, with fishermen traveling greater distances for bigger and better fishing areas. Fishing was often the reason—accidentally or not—for discovering new lands.

AMERICA'S
FIRST INDUSTRY

The plentiful fishing grounds of the North Atlantic brought Europeans westward before 1500. Rick Sorenson's ancestors were among them. In fact, commercial fishing was the first industry of the New World. Muscle and sail moved the ships in those days. And cod was the lure of the Grand Banks of Newfoundland. So numerous were these fish, the Englishman Bartholomew Gosnold, one of the first Europeans to visit New England, named a nearby peninsula Cape Cod in the early 1600s.

Fishermen settling in the New World brought their superstitions with them, since fishing has always been a gamble of sorts. For one thing, it was believed to bring good luck if a fisherman wore one sock correctly, and the other one inside out. Whistling on board was strictly forbidden, for fear of "whistling up" a storm. Times have changed now, and many superstitions are gone. But not all of them. It is possible today to see good luck deer horns sprouting from the mast of a fishing boat—just in case.

FROM WHALING YEARS
TO THE PRESENT

Whaling, too, took its place in history. Whale oil for lamps and candles brought light to people all over the world. Only when oil was discovered in Pennsylvania in 1859 did the need for whale oil decline. Rick's great-great-grandfather, Olaf, was such a whaler, shipping out for months and working with his crew in the Atlantic. When the need for whale oil decreased, Olaf listened to the cry "Westward Ho!" and traveled by covered wagon to California. There he brought his Norwegian ways, showing the fishermen a few special tricks, and learning a few himself.

In the twentieth century, fishing methods advanced. When motors were invented for cars, they were adapted for boats as well. During World War II, the **depth finder** was developed to help locate enemy submarines. Later, when peace came, the same sounders were installed on fishing boats to help search out fish.

THE LAND UNDER THE WATER

Just as the earth blooms in the spring, so does the ocean have its seasons. The sun is the source of energy for water life as well as for land life. Since water covers about 70 percent of the Earth, the ocean uses its share of the energy from the sun.

All living things in the world are nourished by plants or by animals that eat plants. Without plants, living creatures would die. Energy from the sun grows plants which in turn feed living creatures. This is so in the ocean as well as on land.

Oceans, too, have their "mountains," "deserts," and "jungles." The deeper the plants are under the surface, the less chance they have for light. The same is true for plants under cloudy water where light cannot get through as readily. Where sunlight passes through water more easily, sea plants thrive and bloom.

Thus the lands at great depths in the ocean are the "deserts" where no light shines and no energy-giving plants live. Fortunately about 10 percent of underwater land is within 100 feet (30 m) of the surface. Most of this area lies along coasts and is called the **continental shelf.** If you picture a swimming pool in your mind, the continental shelf would be the shallow part of the pool, sloping toward the deep end. Sometimes this shelf of the ocean is narrow, as around Africa. Sometimes it is a flat section which covers miles under the surface, like that off the coast of Newfoundland.

Because the continental shelf is fairly elevated, it receives much light from the sun. Underwater plants and animals grow abundantly there. Since there is plenty of food, the fish come there, too. And who is not far behind?—the fisherman.

WHAT DO FISH EAT?

Fish are plant and meat eaters. The most important plant ingredient for ocean creatures is the microscopic, free-floating plant called **plankton.** This tiny plant is the basic food for *all* marine animal life. Where there are concentrations of plankton, there the fish go. There is also an animal plankton called **zooplankton.**

A slightly more developed form of ocean life is the tiny **krill,** a very small shellfish. It's interesting to note that the largest animal in the world eats one of the smallest animals in the world. The blue whale swallows krill in huge amounts. All told, the whale needs one million calories a day, which is the estimate for what one adult person needs for an entire year.

Plankton are fussy as to where they live. They like the right amount of sunlight, the right temperatures, and a place where there are nutrient salts and minerals in the water. All these elements above the continental shelf blend to bring richness to the seas. Rivers from the land wash nutrients down. Currents and waves mix in oxygen. And the sunlight provides the energy for plankton growth. When two ocean currents meet—like the Gulf Stream and the Labrador Current—they come crashing full on, and stir everything together. The result is a fertile underwater "dinner" rich in food. Plankton are eaten by fish larvae, which in turn are eaten by larger fish, which are eaten by still larger fish, and so on. Most sea creatures do not have much change in their menu—devouring fish and more fish and more fish.

METRIC 1 2

The tiny krill shellfish is a form of animal plankton.

RED TIDES

As important as plankton are, some have their dangerous side, too. Usually during summer or fall, a type of plankton explodes in a tremendous **bloom** which lasts for several weeks. These blooms are brought on by warmth and light from the sun, and certain concentrations of salt and nutrients.

When a bloom occurs, large and small patches of this soupy plant growth appear in the sea, turning the water a variety of red colors. Sometimes the plankton clog fishing nets. The term for this great flowering is called the **red tides.** Under certain conditions, it produces **paralytic shellfish poisoning (PSP).** Dinoflagellates, which produce these poisonous wastes, along with other plankton, form the diet for shellfish and small fish. The poison is taken in by the shellfish, separated and stored by the creature, but does not harm it. However, when contaminated shellfish are eaten by humans, sickness or death can result. After the bloom, shellfish filter out the poison and purify themselves within a short period of time.

It was once believed that shellfish could be eaten only in months that had an ''r'' in them, like March, April, or September. During these times, shellfish were thought to be safe. In truth, there is no way of telling if these seafoods are healthy to eat except by a chemical test.

A MYSTERIOUS SURPRISE

On a summer afternoon a few days before Christmas in 1938, a fishing trawler running the waters off South Africa brought up a net full of fish from 40 fathoms (73 m). Among the catch was an unusual blue creature five feet (1.524 m) long and weighing 127 pounds (58 kg). The captain, never having seen such a fish before, contacted a museum on shore. After investigation, it was determined the fish was a **coelacanth.** This type of fish was thought to be extinct for the past 50 million years! Finding such a species would be like finding a living dinosaur now, in some hidden place on Earth.

The seas have always seemed a mysterious place, one reason being that the underwater world is not people's natural environment. Even scientists have much to learn about underwater life—like the coelacanth making its surprising appearance. Yet much exploration has been done, and most fish have been categorized. Added up, there are about 300 species of commercial fish in the United States, and more than 1,000 worldwide. The commercial fisherman knows what fish he is searching for, and for what purpose they will be used. He also knows where to go to fill his **hold.**

It is difficult to speak of the United States commercial fishing industry without referring to other countries as well. Although fish are generally found in certain areas, they have no railings fencing them in. Hunting them is difficult because of the size of their "backyards" and the fact that they are hidden under the water. Humans cannot spot them as they can deer on land.

WHY FISH STAY NEAR HOME

Some types of fish stay in the same large areas, while others roam the vast oceans. Cod, for instance, can be found near the British Isles, but do not travel much farther south than the Gulf of Maine. In the Atlantic, the bluefin tuna (weighing sometimes 1,800 pounds [810 kg]) swims from Iceland to the Caribbean on the East Coast of the United States. Yet tuna on the West Coast, in the Pacific Ocean, is much smaller in size (about 250 pounds [113 kg]). Herring, which make up the largest part of the world's catch, swim in northern waters, and do not go much farther south than Cape Cod.

Why aren't salmon found off Mexico rather than Alaska? Why are halibut found in deep water rather than swimming near the surface? Besides the natural obstacles of the ocean—the "mountains" and the "deserts,"—two important factors determine where fish find it most comfortable to live. One is temperature.

Just as polar bears enjoy Arctic weather on land, so do salmon like cold, northern seas like those around Taku Inlet where the *Cora Jean* fishes. As lizards thrive in warmer climates, so do tuna enjoy milder water.

In the winter, how cold does it get where you live? How hot during the summer? On land, in some locations, temperatures vary over 130°F (54°C) from one season to another.

Ocean surface temperatures do not change as much from cold to warm as temperatures do on land. They vary on an average between 40 and 80°F (4–27°C). Salt water loses more heat the deeper it becomes, so that ocean depths are cooler than the surface.

The other factor that determines where fish swim is water **salinity,** or the amount of salt in the water. Surface fish can bear a wide degree of salinity changes, while fish in the depths cannot stand much of a difference. Only a few species like salmon can adapt. They live parts of their lives in both fresh water and salt water. Salinity is the reason most ocean fish cannot survive in fresh water, and why freshwater fish stay at home in lakes and rivers.

When Nature changes her habits and does something different, she affects many plants and animals. Near the Equator on the Pacific side of South America, occasionally a northwest wind

WORLD FISHERIES

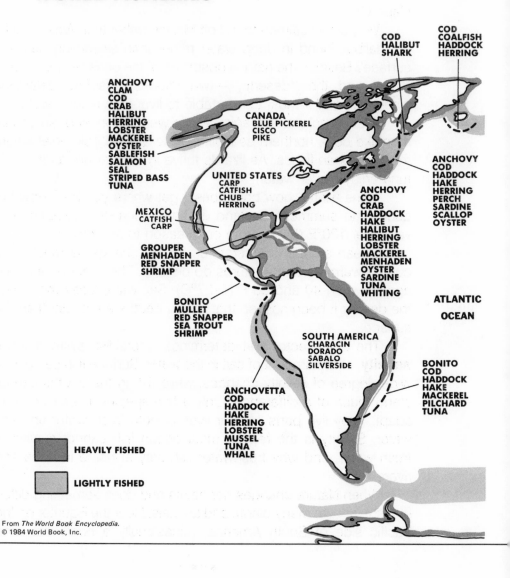

COD
HALIBUT
SHARK

COD
COALFISH
HADDOCK
HERRING

ANCHOVY
CLAM
COD
CRAB
HALIBUT
HERRING
LOBSTER
MACKEREL
OYSTER
SABLEFISH
SALMON
SEAL
STRIPED BASS
TUNA

CANADA
BLUE PICKEREL
CISCO
PIKE

ANCHOVY
COD
HADDOCK
HAKE
HERRING
PERCH
SARDINE
SCALLOP
OYSTER

UNITED STATES
CARP
CATFISH
CHUB
HERRING

ANCHOVY
COD
CRAB
HADDOCK
HAKE
HALIBUT
HERRING
LOBSTER
MACKEREL
MENHADEN
OYSTER
SARDINE
TUNA
WHITING

MEXICO
CATFISH
CARP

GROUPER
MENHADEN
RED SNAPPER
SHRIMP

ATLANTIC

OCEAN

BONITO
MULLET
RED SNAPPER
SEA TROUT
SHRIMP

SOUTH AMERICA
CHARACIN
DORADO
SABALO
SILVERSIDE

BONITO
COD
HADDOCK
HAKE
MACKEREL
PILCHARD
TUNA

ANCHOVETTA
COD
HADDOCK
HAKE
HERRING
LOBSTER
MUSSEL
TUNA
WHALE

HEAVILY FISHED

LIGHTLY FISHED

From *The World Book Encyclopedia.*
© 1984 World Book, Inc.

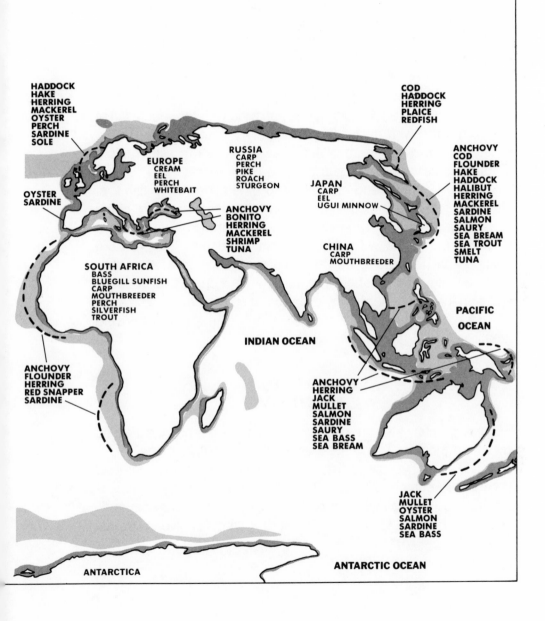

HADDOCK
HAKE
HERRING
MACKEREL
OYSTER
PERCH
SARDINE
SOLE

COD
HADDOCK
HERRING
PLAICE
REDFISH

EUROPE
CREAM
EEL
PERCH
WHITEBAIT

RUSSIA
CARP
PERCH
PIKE
ROACH
STURGEON

JAPAN
CARP
EEL
UGUI MINNOW

ANCHOVY
COD
FLOUNDER
HAKE
HADDOCK
HALIBUT
HERRING
MACKEREL
SARDINE
SALMON
SAURY
SEA BREAM
SEA TROUT
SMELT
TUNA

OYSTER
SARDINE

ANCHOVY
BONITO
HERRING
MACKEREL
SHRIMP
TUNA

CHINA
CARP
MOUTHBREEDER

SOUTH AFRICA
BASS
BLUEGILL SUNFISH
CARP
MOUTHBREEDER
PERCH
SILVERFISH
TROUT

PACIFIC
OCEAN

INDIAN OCEAN

ANCHOVY
FLOUNDER
HERRING
RED SNAPPER
SARDINE

ANCHOVY
HERRING
JACK
MULLET
SALMON
SARDINE
SAURY
SEA BASS
SEA BREAM

JACK
MULLET
OYSTER
SALMON
SARDINE
SEA BASS

ANTARCTICA

ANTARCTIC OCEAN

blows warm water toward shore farther south than usual. The lack of salt in these incoming waters, coupled with the rise in temperature when they mix with the colder, fertile waters of the coast, are too much for the normal plankton structure. The result is disastrous. These changes kill the plankton. In turn, millions of fish that feed on plankton die, as well as the birds that feed on the fish.

By and large, salinity affects the eggs of fish more than it does the adults. If a fish approaches an area with too much salt, it can turn and swim away. Eggs, however, floating freely in the water, cannot direct themselves away from such a salty region. Eggs in tremendous numbers are killed this way.

Water pressure and currents also determine where fish live. Fish from great depths could not survive the lesser pressure of the surface shallows. If a grenadier fish is brought up from nearly a mile down, its eyes will explode from its sockets. The pressure changes are too great. Larvae from shellfish, free-floating near surface water, are crushed if, when the time comes for them to settle on the ocean floor, they drop too deeply. Currents, because of their movement, help distribute younger fish about their living area.

WHERE FISH
LIKE TO LIVE

Excluding freshwater species, ocean fish are generally classified by where they are found: coastal, offshore, and deep-sea.

Coastal fish and shellfish, the largest group, range near land from frozen coasts to tropical beaches. Included in their number are herring, cod, halibut, pollock, salmon, menhaden, mackeral, crab, and shrimp. About 80 percent of marine fish live in coastal areas.

Marine offshore fish range farther from the coast, and live in the upper 600 feet (183 m) of the surface. Some of the larger game fish are found there—tuna, marlin, and swordfish. Sharks also roam through those vast regions.

Deep-sea fish swim in an area below the 600-foot level far out into the ocean. Pressure there can be 100 times greater than at the surface. Deep-sea fish die at the lighter pressure near the surface.

At the layer below 600 feet, the fish are usually small (six inches [15 cm]) and practically all produce a glowing light of some kind. Lanternfish and certain eels inhabit this zone.

Below the 3,000-foot [915 m] level—that is more than one-half mile down—the midnight region begins. Food is scarce there. Species in this zone include the rattails and anglers.

Inland waters are much smaller than saltwater oceans. They are the freshwater ponds, swamps, streams, rivers, and lakes, which do not have the salt content of the open seas. Fish of fresh waters include catfish, carp, pike, trout, char, bass, sturgeon, and whitefish, to name a few. Some of these species are popular with the sport fisherman. Like saltwater creatures, freshwater fish live in warm or cold waters and at different depths.

One species, the sturgeon, is overfished and in danger of disappearing. Its eggs are used for caviar, a very expensive appetizer. In some places, caviar sells for as high as $800 per pound.

Fish caught in fresh waters do not make up a large part of the United States commercial fish industry. Other countries catch slightly more fish from their inland waters.

Some fish, like salmon, migrating trouts, chars, and shads, are born in fresh water, live their adult lives in salt water, and return to fresh water to lay their eggs. No one knows exactly how the fish find their way back to the same stream they were born in after swimming around the ocean. They have no roads or maps to guide them. Some scientists say it is because these fish have a special smelling sense which gives them direction. In any case, they seem to have a built-in homing sense which takes them back to the very freshwater area of their birth, often only a few hundred yards from where they were hatched. It is one of the mysteries of life.

WHY FISH ARE IMPORTANT

Every year more people are born into the world. And every thirty-five years the population doubles itself. In some countries, there are more people than can be fed properly, and some of them are starving because they do not have enough to eat. Since people are taking up more room on land, less land is left for farming. As a result, less food is grown when more food is needed. Fish are an important source of food for the people of the world.

One reason fish are valuable to the human diet is that their bodies are packed with protein. This nutrient builds and repairs skin, muscles, and tissue, and keeps the body in good health. Without protein, humans waste away. Such a lack of protein in the body is less likely to occur in nations along the sea where people eat fish regularly. Foods such as pork, beef, and poultry also con-

This chum salmon will never make it upstream to reproduce. Unseen, several other fish struggle against the white water at the base of the falls.

tain protein, but in some countries such meats are not close at hand. And some people cannot afford them. Fish is often available, and adds a nice variety to the human diet—as well as being healthful.

Besides protein, fish contain high levels of vitamins, fats, and minerals. Vitamin A, found in fish, promotes good eyesight and helps keep the body resistant to infections. Vitamin D helps build and maintain healthy bones and teeth.

Not just people benefit from fish. If you have ever watched ducks dive in a lake, or have seen pictures of eagles swooping down to the sea, or bears eating salmon along a river, you can understand that other creatures thrive on fish as well. It would be hard to imagine what life would be like if there were no fish in the world.

2

HOW FISH ARE CAUGHT

The mountains backing Taku Harbor were veiled in mist. Rick's father, Dave, cut the motor to idle, and the *Cora Jean* slowed and drifted on the tide. The gill net was wound firmly around the large stern drum.

Dave called from the bridge. "Okay, son. We'll keep her at four knots."

The engine revved, and the *Cora Jean* began chugging in a wide circle.

Rick threw the buoy end of the net into the water and watched the net peel from the drum. Eventually, a net wall would drift in the water, with floats along the top and a lead line keeping the bottom down. This was a salmon drift net, which meant that the holes in the net were big enough to catch the head of a salmon. The net string caught the gills of the fish so that it could not escape. Smaller fish swam right through. The new **monofilament line** was very strong and could carry a heavy load of fish without breaking.

At last, Rick heard the dull whop as the boat end of the net tightened. The net wall—about a quarter-mile (0.4 km) long—was soon drifting upright in the water, only buoys and the corks visible.

Facing the bridge, Rick shouted, "How long should we keep her down, Dad?"

"Two hours, maybe. If there's no action, we'll check the radio and see what Walt's up to."

Rick shoved his hands in his pockets and settled down for the long wait, gazing at the net strung out behind the boat.

FISHING GEAR

A net such as the one Rick was using has remained unchanged since earliest recorded history. Even though fishing goes back to prehistoric times, the essential methods for catching fish are not much different today. Hooks, lines, nets, traps—gear used by Indians and ancient Egyptians—are used in the 1980s. The methods are shared by all countries of the world. When a new monofilament netting was developed, the tribes of Madagascar adopted it as well as did American fishermen. The Republic of South Africa uses fishing gear from California. Worldwide organizations such as the Food and Agriculture Organization (FAO) of the United Nations afford close contacts for fishermen of most countries.

Whereas a sport fisherman casts his line for enjoyment, the commercial fisherman sells his catch to make a living. It is a business, a livelihood for the commercial fisherman. He is ever aware of new fishing grounds, new tools, and new methods that will increase his landings and improve his sales.

Rick's boat, the *Cora Jean*, is a combination boat, which means it is used for different kinds of fishing during the year. In

May, the boat **longlines** for halibut. In this case, the stern drum reels out a long line to the sea floor. Along sections **(skates)** of this groundline are hung shorter lines or **leaders (gangions)** which carry baited hooks at the ends. At each end of the groundline is a vertical anchored line which runs to a buoy on the surface. (Japanese fishermen lay lines sometimes 75 miles [121 km] long.) Often more than one longline is set side by side with another. These strings of longlines are left on the bottom to "soak"— sometimes for twenty-four hours or more. A **hydraulic** system helps pull the line in, because, if the harvest is good, the line is heavy with fish. A fisherman must be careful when the big halibut are being pulled into the boat, for a flip of a 100-pound (45 km) halibut's tail can break a person's leg. The fish are **gaffed,** released from the hook, and put in a holder before icing.

In November, the *Cora Jean* takes on another job. She loads her deck with pots and goes out king-crab fishing. Rick is in school at that time, but his father takes a couple of deckhands along to help.

In the crab fishery, a piece of squid or rotten fish is placed in a nylon-cord or stainless-steel net pot. The opening at one end allows the crab to crawl in, but it cannot get out. The pot is on a line that is lowered to the sea floor, while the other end is attached to a buoy. On the East Coast, lobsters are caught this way.

When the *Cora Jean* fishes this shellfish, her hold is filled with seawater. It is a law that crabs be kept alive while at sea, so the boat hold must carry salt water.

On boats larger than the *Cora Jean,* the pots may be rectangular-shaped and weigh more than 800 pounds (363 km) apiece. When a big company fishes by this method, whole strings of pots may be laid out on the ocean floor, some with as many as 100 pots each. In such operations, the pots are reeled in, emptied, and put out again right away. In a very large operation, over a period of

Live king crabs are off-loaded
from one boat to another.

ten hours, a good crew can haul and reset as many as 300 pots. Crabbing is a popular industry, for crabs bring in a lot of money per pound.

At times Dave Sorenson "sets" gill nets, too. With this system, he anchors a net in the water by using two long poles at either end. It looks much like an underwater volleyball net.

Set nets of Nova Scotia, Canada, have a special problem. There the area has extreme tidewater action (rising and dropping over 25 feet (8 m) in a twelve-hour period). Because of this, the nets have to be set on very long poles under water. When the tide goes out, the fishermen have to climb ladders to reach the nets and pick out the captured fish.

PURSE SEINING

Though the *Cora Jean* is adaptable, she cannot do everything. Several important types of fishing are handled by other methods.

Over half of the total United States fish catch is landed by **purse seining.** Purse seines are used to catch small fish that tend to school in open water—herring, menhaden, anchovy. The net, run out from the boat, balloons open. When a school of fish is trapped within, the bottom is drawn closed like a purse. The net and fish are then hauled aboard the vessel.

Menhaden, a small fish that is the most caught fish in the United States, is captured in such a manner. On the Atlantic Coast, two small purse-seine boats are carried to the fishing grounds aboard a large ship. At a likely spot, the two small craft, each with half the long purse-seine net aboard, are lowered into the water from the mother boat. The vessels travel along until a school of menhaden is spotted, and then the crafts speed apart and play the net into the water until they surround the school.

Finally, the bottom is drawn shut so the fish cannot escape underneath. Part of the net is hauled up by hand or power block. The large ship then comes by and the load is either scooped aboard the bigger ship, or a hose and pump suck up the fish and make the transfer. Since menhaden are used for industrial products, they are not cared for as carefully as are food fish.

Such fishing with smaller boats can be dangerous during rough weather. But they are greatly efficient—fast and maneuverable.

TRAWLING

Fishing by trawl is the most widely used method in the entire world. Both the purse seine and the trawl can be operated in fresh water as well as salt water.

With **trawling** gear, an open cone-shaped net bag is dragged behind a boat. Fish are caught within this bag whether the net is dragged along the bottom or pulled along at lesser depths. It is like a giant fish with a big mouth that gulps cod, flounder, shrimp, haddock, pollock, whiting, hake, and other fish as it plows through the sea. Eventually, the narrow or tubular end (cod end) of the bag fills with fish, and the net is hauled aboard the ship. A skipper on the surface cannot tell when a bag is full. But by viewing electronic instruments on the bridge, he has a fair idea.

At times, trawl skippers use two boats in trawling. American Indians before Columbus fished this way using rowboats, especially for salmon. In modern days, each boat, running at a similar speed on a parallel route, carries a cable which tows the bag. To use this system—**pair trawling**—the catch must be profitable enough to financially support two boats doing the job.

Sometimes surprises come up from the deep, like the coelacanth.

In the first half of the twentieth century, Gulf of Mexico fishermen dragged offshore areas for white shrimp. At the end of one day in 1950, the Salvador brothers of Florida thought they would put down their trawl one last time before going home. To their surprise, the nets came up filled with *pink* shrimp. The pinks had just come out of their muddy beds for night feeding. Fishermen working during the day had not even known that they were there. The brothers tried to keep the secret, but others soon found out, and the area became a night-fishing bonanza.

Today, more money is made in the United States from shrimp supplied in large part by Gulf of Mexico fishermen, than from any other sea creature.

TROLLING

If you were to stand on the stern of a boat, throw a baited hook on a line into the water, and hold onto the pole while the craft moved slowly on through the water, you would be **trolling.** Salmon troll boats have two or more long poles extending at angles off the sides of the boat. From these, stainless-steel fishing lines trail into the water. Where the line runs from the pole outward, bells are mounted to alert the fisherman when a fish has taken the hook. Fish taken by this method are usually in good condition and command a high price at sale.

Albacore-tuna trolling is less complex than salmon trolling. Tuna is a surface-swimming ocean fish. In contrast to the large superseiners sailing out of California, smaller troll-fishing boats simply put out a pole with a short line and a barbless hook. Live bait is thrown over the side; the tuna feed in a frenzy—even to the point of biting off a person's finger if his hand is in the water. In the stern, men snag the tuna and flip the 20-pounders (9 kg) into a pit. These fish are easily removed from the barbless hooks, and the

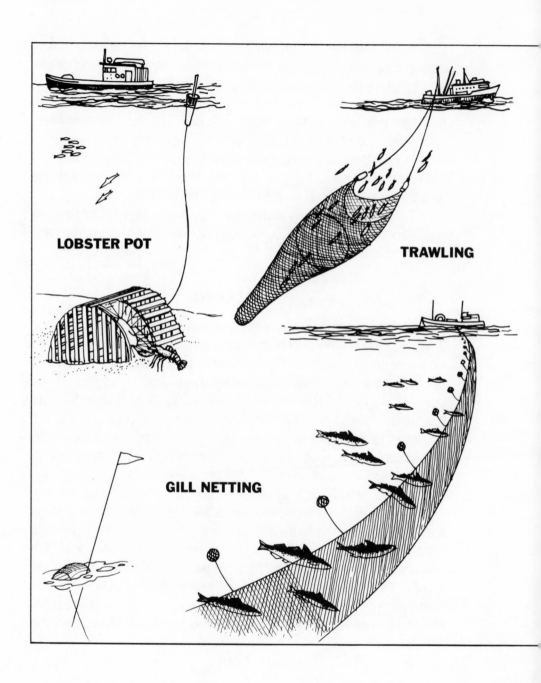

LOBSTER POT

TRAWLING

GILL NETTING

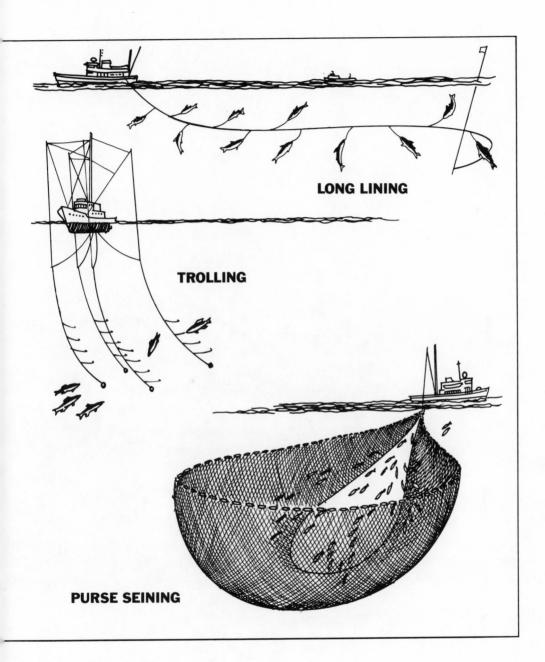

LONG LINING

TROLLING

PURSE SEINING

Trolling for salmon

lines are quickly returned to the water. Sometimes, in one hour, a dozen men can fish 20 tons of tuna aboard. A ship may wander for weeks in search of a school, but, once found, the fish go crazy eating the bait. Just as quickly, they may dive and disappear.

Besides the fishing methods mentioned above, other systems are used: **weir traps, trammel nets, shellfish dredges, tongs, spears, harpoons,** and **scoop nets.** These, however, do not add substantially to United States commercial landings.

SPECIAL HELP
FOR THE FISHERMAN

From sail, to steam, to gasoline and diesel engines, fishing has advanced. Today United States commercial fishing takes place on the smallest 16-foot (5 m) skiff to the largest tuna superseiner extending 300 feet (91 m) from bow to stern—the length of a football field.

The 1900s brought an increased use of hydraulic power. Such a system was applied to the seine drum that set out and hauled in the net, saving the backs of many a fisherman. Nylon line and nets, too, have gone a long way to giving a boost to the net fisheries.

Fishing has always been hard work. Yet few mariners will disagree that the one great invention that did more to help the lot of the net fishermen was the **Puretic Power Block.**

Mario Puretic came to the United States from Yugoslavia. Arriving finally in California, he shippped aboard boats fishing for sardine and anchovy. He was not the first one who experienced the hard labor of hauling in loaded fish nets by hand. It took eight to ten men to work a salmon seine.

But Puretic did something about the hard work, designing a power block which would haul seine nets out of the water with a rope-driven block. Even though experiments were successful, no one would give money to back the inventor. Finally, in 1955, a Seattle firm took interest. The company was the first to develop a hydraulic unit weighing less than 200 pounds (91kg). Before long, orders poured in, and eventually the power block was put into use around the world. The United Nations estimates that almost half of all commercially caught fish have been taken aboard with the power block.

LEARNING UNDERWATER SECRETS WITH ELECTRONICS

If you were 6 feet (183 cm) tall, standing in a rowboat on the ocean, you would be able to see only as far as about 3 miles (5 km) because of the curvature of the earth. If you were 30 feet (9 m) up on the bridge of a boat, you could stretch your sight to about 6 miles (10 m). Boats would be visible, along with fish—if they were jumping above the surface. But everything under the water would be hidden. To help the fisherman find his way in bad weather, and to detect fish under the surface, electronic aids were developed. Now almost any object can be spotted above or below the water.

One of the most important pieces of equipment on a boat is the radio. Tuning in, a fisherman is able to get weather reports, hear the news, and be alerted to emergencies. When a skipper finds a good fishing area, he may want to share it with his friends. Speaking plainly over the radio would alert everyone listening, and they in turn would speed to the fishing grounds and fish it out. So he tries to keep the hot spots to himself. Even radio scramblers have been installed on some vessels so that only friends can tune in and be understood.

*A purse seine of herring is
pulled aboard. Notice how the power block,
(above), helps the fisherman lift the load.*

If David Sorenson on the *Cora Jean* hit a hot spot at Taku Harbor, and was catching nets full of fish, he would call his friend Walt on the *Katy Jo* and tell him—in code. Long beforehand, they would have both agreed that if either of them mentioned the word *bucket* over the radio, the other should come, because the fishing would be great. They would tell the location by code, too. The conversation might go something like this:

Dave: *Katy Jo.* You got her on there? *Cora Jean* here.

Walt: Sure thing, *Cora Jean.* Got you fine. How's it going?

Dave: Pretty slow, Walt. Real slow. Just got her picked up here, and looking for a little open stretch.

Walt: Nothing here either. Was hoping you'd have a hot fish report for me.

Dave: No way. Man, I've had it. I haven't had a decent set all morning. I even knocked my deck bucket overboard. What a disaster.

Walt: Tough luck, man. Say, where are you anyway?

Dave: Oh, you remember where I was last week when the sea lion went through my net? I'm about two miles above that.

Walt: Well, hope it picks up pretty soon. I might see you on the way in.

Dave: Sure thing. See you later.

Not all boats are fitted with a variety of electrical equipment. If a fisherman can afford a few fish-finding devices, like the ones mentioned on page 32, his catch may increase.

This two-person minisub was loaned to the Alaska Department of Fish and Game for commercial fishing research.

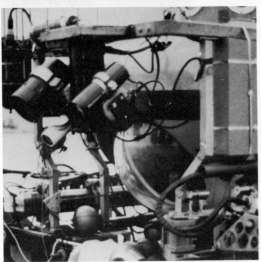

Because the sub cruises the "midnight deep," it is equipped with floodlights, sonar instruments, cameras, and mechanical arms. The space inside is cramped. Enough oxygen is carried to enable the sub to remain underwater for three days.

Depth or **echo sounders** are fish-detecting devices. Originally, they were used during World War II to locate enemy submarines. With the use of sound impulses, which bounce off rocks, schools of fish, and other obstacles, fish can be found. Since the advent of the data-processing age, color-video sounders are being developed, with readouts showing colors which help to distinguish the kinds of fish beneath. Because the video sounder is computer-based, there are no moving parts, no belts to be repaired.

Whether vessels come equipped with the latest electrical gear or not, boats nevertheless need navigational aids. When the weather is bad, the skipper must find his way home safely.

An **autopilot** directs the boat automatically. A **magnetometer** senses when the boat is going off a set course, and will automatically bring it back on.

For locating ship position on the ocean, boats use a **radio direction finder** (loran). This device measures the time difference between the arrivals of two radio signals from two known stations. By referring to a loran chart and intersecting these signal points, the skipper can establish his own location. The *Cora Jean* has both a loran and an automatic pilot.

When a captain cannot see ahead, he uses his **radar**. Radio waves are sent out, and bounce off objects ahead. The time between the signal being sent out and its recorded return gives the distance to the object. Radar antennae can be pointed in any direction to obtain a reading. Such a device helps the skipper navigate as well as avoid collision with other ships.

Large ships like tuna superseiners have the latest instruments. Such would include radios, radar, depth sounder/recorders, plus more. In addition, several are equipped with helicopter pads, as more and more use is being made of aircraft as aids in spotting fish. Eventually satellites may be used to accomplish the same purpose—finding the fish.

3

WHAT WE CATCH

Several hours before, Rick Sorenson had released the gill net and let it drift in the water. Since then, the boat had made several passes, and Rick had seen the fish caught in the mesh below the surface. Now he took the long gaff, hooked the end of the net line, and attached it to the stern drum. With rubber gloves on, and his father on the other side of the reel, Rick stepped on the long pedal at his feet. The drum rolled, took up slack net, and the fish began appearing from the water.

Both father and son worked with practiced ease, releasing the salmon from the mesh. Once freed, the reds, as they are sometimes called, were pitched into large plastic tubs nearby.

"Hey!" Rick cried suddenly, stepping back from the foot pedal.

The drum stopped. There, struggling against the net, flapped a small shark. It must not have been caught tightly, for a vigorous flip tore the net, and the shark dropped back into the water.

"Sharks!" Dave snorted in disgust, examining the net. "What a pain."

Before long the net cleared the water. The fish were dumped from the tubs into the slush of the hold.

"Not bad," said Dave. "About thirty sockeyes. What say we put her down again, and then head in?"

"Go back—so soon?"

Dave grinned. "You think your mother would ever forgive us if we missed her birthday tomorrow? We'll go out again later this week." He motioned to the cabin. "How about making us sandwiches while I reel this out again."

Ten minutes later Rick walked out to the stern where his father stood. Dave took the sandwich Rick handed him, and had most of it down in three bites. Suddenly he laughed, sputtering with a half-full mouth.

Rick tipped his head, smiling. "What's wrong, Dad? What's so funny?"

"The fish . . . " Dave began. "Here we've got"—he swallowed—"maybe 400 pounds of salmon in the hold." He swallowed again, shaking his head. "It struck me funny. All that salmon, and you make tuna-fish sandwiches!"

Rick saw the humor, and couldn't help but grin himself.

FROM WATER TO PLATE

There is no way of knowing for sure, but it might be fair to guess that everyone in the United States has tried, or eaten, a tuna or salmon sandwich at some time in his or her life. And that is what most processed and imported fish are used for—food. Tuna, salmon, shellfish, sardines, mackeral, rockfishes—are all popular varieties.

Compared with those in other countries, Americans eat a fair amount of seafood. In 1982, an American ate about 12 pounds (5 kg) of fish and seafood during the year. A person from Japan or Iceland ate about four times that amount. Still, the United States's consumption per person is quite a bit more than the lowest, eaten by a person from Afghanistan, who consumed less than a pound (0.45 kg).

Americans, like the rest of the world, prefer fresh and frozen fish. Freezing has made it possible for fish to be brought to shore in excellent condition, and has boosted fish sales in supermarkets. In addition, the growth of fast-food restaurant chains offering fishburgers has added new life to the industry.

OTHER USES FOR FISH

Fish not eaten by humans, and waste materials from processed fish, are used in several ways. For one, the fish are ground up for meal and fed to farm animals. Using fish this way is nothing new. Marco Polo in the fourteenth century reported dried fish being fed to cows, sheep, camels, and horses in some Asian countries.

Poultry, too, benefits from fish meal, which is rich in protein, nitrogen, and phosphorus—enabling the industry to raise bigger, healthier birds. Menhaden, America's main catch from both the Gulf and Atlantic coasts, is processed for fish meal. And the United States buys fish meal from other countries as well.

In addition, fish are added to pet food; oils derived from them are mixed in paint and margarine; skins are used for glue or for a gel to clarify wine; shark and other fish skins are tanned into leather; and waste is ground into fertilizer.

If you have ever owned a tortoise-shell comb, or pearls, or coral jewelry, you have used products from the sea. Mussel shells are cut for buttons; sponges are dried for cleaning purposes.

The harvest of the ocean serves other purposes. Studies are

being conducted to see if migrating salmon can give some clues to the aging process in humans. In another area, freshwater carp may help point to a solution for diabetes. Fishing supports many fields, and promises to contribute to even more in the future.

WHY DOES
THE UNITED STATES
BUY FISH?

Most of the world's fish catches, too, are for food. By the early 1980s, the United States ranked fourth in the world for total commercial fish and seafood landings. Only Japan, Russia, and China caught more fish. About 10 percent of the total world's catch came from fresh water.

Fish caught by United States fishermen are not enough for American demands. Thus the United States buys (imports) fish products from other countries. There are two reasons why other countries are able to sell fish to the United States. One, the governments of nations like Russia give money to their fishing industries to buy large factory ships and to pay their expenses for traveling around the world. The government actually owns the ships. In the United States, fishermen have to buy their own boats and pay their own expenses. The United States fisherman must sell his fish for more money in order to cover the expenses he has.

The second reason the United States imports fish products is that some other countries, such as Japan, employ their fishermen for less money than Americans can work for. Therefore, fish items produced by a few foreign nations cost less.

At the same time, countries like Japan buy American fish products such as salmon and salmon roe (eggs) because Japanese people like them, and because Japan cannot produce enough of these items itself.

Halibut is off-loaded to the cold-storage
building on the dock at Sitka, Alaska.

HOW MANY
AMERICANS FISH?

It is difficult to obtain a count of all the workers in the United States fishing industry. Because manufacturing workers are usually employed in one specific job, a count of cannery or food-processing people is possible. Fishermen are a different story. Some work a few months a year, some work one day a week, others work year round, switching from one type of fishing to another, as Dave Sorenson does. Dave gill nets for salmon in the summer, king crabs in November, tanner crabs in February, and longlines for halibut in May. If he were counted for each fishery, he would be four people. Many fishermen do this, combining several types of fisheries in order to work the year around and earn enough money to support their families.

As to actual figures, the National Marine Fisheries Service estimates that a total of 302,600 people (197,900 fishermen, 104,700 food processing workers) were employed in the United States fishing business in 1981.

Seen as a whole, fishing does not employ many people in the United States. Other industries such as construction, government, services, and trade employ many more. Yet in port cities like Cameron, Louisiana; Gloucester, Massachusetts; Beaufort-Morehead City, North Carolina; Kodiak, Alaska; Astoria, Oregon; and Monterey, California, much of the community life revolves around fishing.

Fishing also boosts other industries and agencies. For example, fish are shipped (transportation), sold in supermarkets (retail trade), and in restaurants (trade and services); money changes hands (finance); laws are made (government).

The industry of fishing is bound to expand. With planning, perhaps the ocean harvest can help fill the gap between population and food needs for the years to come.

4

FISHING
AS A
BUSINESS

The clouds hung heavy and wet over Taku Inlet as the *Cora Jean* cut along toward Cooper Point on a course back to town. Rain pelted the water, and white caps foamed the waves. Rounding Jaw Point toward Stephens Passage, a gust of wind tilted the boat to starboard for a moment, and then it swung back.

In the hold of the *Cora Jean,* the salmon swayed with each plunge of the boat, rocking on a bed of slush ice. Dave Sorenson had found this cooling method a sure and easy way of keeping the catch fresh. Each time the *Cora Jean* went out to fish, Dave had the cold storage company lower a hose and fill the hold with three tons (2 t) of ice. With water added, the ice became slush. When the fish were thrown in, they settled to a comfortable level but did not get crushed by the weight of the fish on top. The slush stayed at a safe 32°F (0°C). Later the fish were delivered to the cold storage in town, as fresh as if they were just picked from the net.

Topside, under shelter, Dave held the wheel, steering first one way, then back the other with each toss of the boat. At eye level, the windshield wiper wheezed, pushing to keep the glass clear. Rick stood behind his father, his gaze straight ahead.

"See that everything's nailed down, will you Rick?" asked Dave. "Looks like the ride in is going to be a rough one."

HOW FISH ARE KEPT FRESH

In the early days of history, fishermen had no way of obtaining ice such as the Sorensons do. Instead, boats fished near shore. Their catches were eaten within a day or two. Since fishermen have traveled farther from shore for different species, it has become necessary to preserve the catch in some way. For years, salt served this purpose.

Today fishermen use two basic methods of preserving fish while on the water—ice and refrigeration.

Icing is an efficient method, but a bulky one. The farther away from port a fishermen has to travel, the more ice he must carry. In turn, carrying more ice lessens the space for fish. And the ice itself must be flaked or crushed to the right size: even large ice chips can bruise fish. In this system, crushed ice is layered between the fish. If the fish is large, it is often iced in the gutted body cavity as well.

Although icing does have disadvantages, it keeps the catch fresh for about ten to twelve days. It is a fast system, and the cost is low. Instead of icing, some fishermen fill a hold with water and ice to make slush, just as Dave Sorenson does.

Refrigeration—the process of using a chemical and an energy source to keep things cold—was developed during the early part of this century. Clarence Birdseye, an American inventor, improved one device after another until he created a workable refrigeration system.

After World War II, when the giant stern trawlers roamed the seas, refrigeration took a leap forward. With this process, vessels could fish in distant waters, staying on the fishing grounds for months at a time and still bring in fish in top condition. A refrigeration unit takes up less space than ice, so there is more room in the hold for fish. But it is a costly system; it burns up more energy, and it is a big expense for a small boat owner.

Whether large or small, every boat has unspoken rules the fisherman follows when handling fish: gut, bleed, and wash the fish as soon as possible; avoid rough treatment; be sure both handlers and holds are clean; and chill the catch in some manner as soon as possible.

HOW FISH ARE PREPARED FOR THE MARKET

Once a boat makes it to the dock, the cold-storage company that off-loads the catch might buy the fish and sell it to restaurants or supermarkets fresh, or it might be handled in some other way. The fish might be processed right on a factory vessel immediately after being caught. Whether on shore or at sea, fish may be processed in different ways. The three basic methods are curing, canning, or freezing.

CURING

Curing fish involves drying, salting, smoking, or pickling. No one knows how those methods developed, but humans learned of them over the centuries. Methods vary according to species.

Although sun drying was probably one of the first methods of preserving fish, it is not now used commercially in the United States. Eskimos and Indians still dry fish on outside racks for their personal use. Dehydration, or machine drying, is an important process for other foods—raisins, milk, tomatoes, fruits—but not for seafood. However, some other nations of the world—Japan for one—consider dried fish important.

Salting has long been an efficient and popular preservation technique and is also used as a step in the smoking process. Salt in itself draws out the moisture from the flesh, causing the fish to dry out. Less moisture slows germ growth. Yet salting flavors the meat, and not all people take to the taste.

After a few months in a salt solution, fish may be smoked. To finish this procedure, the salmon, for instance, is soaked in fresh water for three days. It may then be hot smoked, which means it is cooked, or cold smoked, which means it is air dried slightly, smoked, and given a glaze of oil. It then is eaten as it is. Smoked salmon is a popular topping for crackers.

Pickling simply means preserving in a solution of brine or vinegar, like pickles from the store. A small portion of the herring catch is preserved in this manner.

CANNING

Napoleon Bonaparte (1769–1821) of France encouraged the development of canning. He wanted a better way for his supply trains to carry food faster and farther to his armies away from home. Thus he offered a prize for an idea that would help. In 1804 a French candymaker invented a way of preserving food in a jar, and won the prize. From this effort, over the years, the modern can evolved.

Canning is the process of preserving food in an airtight con-

Final inspection of canned salmon before sealing

tainer. Fish are brought to a cannery on shore, processed, packed, labeled, and sent out to supermarkets. On large processing ships, fish are canned right on the fishing grounds.

With the use of tin cans, seafood can be kept nourishing, tasteful, and safe. Tin cans can be sent anywhere in the world, or saved on the kitchen shelf for the next shrimp salad.

FREEZING

Freezing fish right on board a vessel developed after World War II. Since freezing enabled boats to stay away from port longer, the boat design focused on spacious storage capacity rather than on speed. Larger boats were needed for this, and factory vessels evolved.

Usually the fish are frozen whole or filleted (bones removed) into single fillets or frozen blocks. They are sorted, washed in a chilled water bath, gutted, headed, skinned, deboned, and hand checked. Fillets are usually hand packed according to how they will be sold. Fillet blocks (cod, pollock) are packed in trays with no air between layers. Individual fillets are usually quick frozen and then packed in consumer-size containers.

Once frozen products reach land, they are either processed further, sold whole, or boxed and labeled, and finally distributed to retail outlets.

FLOATING CANNERIES

Though the British designed the first stern trawler and used it off the Grand Banks of Newfoundland in the Atlantic Ocean after World War II, Russia and Japan have brought this development to a questionable extreme.

Often having to fish far from home, these giants bring every-

*Its deck bins brimming with groundfish,
a Japanese factory ship works the
Bering Sea area near the Arctic Ocean.
The ship, about two city blocks long,
is supplied by ten catcher boats.*

thing with them. On board they have hospital, repair, recreation, and fuel departments, plus large storage and processing facilities. A few of the vessels are several football fields in length. In one day, a Russian factory ship is able to salt tons of herring; process tons of fish into fish meal; fillet and freeze tons of bottom fish; and manufacture tons of ice, distilled water, and fish oil.

Each year Japan sends a fleet of factory ships for tuna in the Gulf of Mexico. This fleet can catch, process, and send tuna back to the United States for less money than Americans can. Such ships, while they are efficient and waste nothing, have been called the "vacuum cleaners" of the deep, for they sweep the ocean of every living creature in their path—to the point of overfishing.

WATER FARMS

The business of fishing does not just involve processing creatures from the open seas. Another business deals with water farms such as hatcheries, close to shore or on inland waters. Just as agriculture is farming on land, **aquaculture** is farming in water. In this method, sea creatures are grown and developed under human guidance.

Such an idea began centuries ago. Ancient Greeks and Romans raised fish in ponds. A king in India over 2,000 years ago passed a law that his fish were not to be killed during certain times

This hatchery at Little Port Walter, Alaska, incubates thousands of king and coho salmon eggs and fry (recently hatched fish) each year. Salmon eggs are fertilized with milt from a male.

of the year (spawning season). Regulations were part of fishing even at that time. Oysters, also, were cultivated in the Orient several thousands of years ago.

Aquaculture deals with increasing the number of water animals by breeding, feeding, harvesting, caring for the young, and providing for a healthy environment. With special food, fish farmers encourage the fish to grow faster and larger than they would in their normal open waters. In a hatchery, the fish are protected from larger, preying fish, and survive in greater numbers.

Not all fish can be cultured on water farms. Fish like herring, which need lots of room for swimming, do not do well. On the other hand, carp, oysters, shrimp, trout, and catfish can be crowded together, and are important aquaculture species.

At the present time, Japan is growing salmon in a hatchery situation. The Japanese government takes good care of its sea creatures. It even has a fish hospital in Toba Bay. If necessary, the staff makes house calls to fish farms in the area.

Water creatures can be farmed on freshwater lakes and ponds, too. Swamps and tidal areas that are not now farmed might be in the years to come. The Chinese use rice fields which are under shallow water. In the future, many more areas could be developed as water farms.

5

STORMY PROBLEMS
FOR
THE FISHERMAN

The *Cora Jean* pitched in 6-foot (1.82 km) seas, heading toward Bishop Point. Wind funneled between the mountains and roared onto the open water of Stephens Passage.

Inside the cabin, Rick braced against the forward door. Dave kept the bow headed into the waves as best he could, but the ship seemed to sail a course of its own. Water washed over the bow and pounded against the windows. At times it was hard seeing 5 feet (1.52 km) beyond the rail.

"Once we reach the channel, we'll be all right," shouted Dave over the outside noise.

Rick answered, peering ahead. "Can't be sure, but I think that's Bishop coming up."

"According to the compass, you're right on."

Dave forced the boat to port, and felt it strain against the blasting storm. The *Cora Jean* shuddered, but obeyed, making little headway. She cut the waves, riding the swell like a bucking horse.

Finally clearing a jutting of rocks, Dave brought the boat sharply to starboard, and the tension broke. The vessel veered from the storm and rode with the wind, sweeping into Gastineau Channel.

A few minutes more, and the *Cora Jean* relaxed, taking a slower roll, a smoother glide. She sped down the way, the wind at her stern, her bow pointed to home.

ALWAYS THE WEATHER

*"TWO ATLANTIC COAST TRAWLERS
RUN INTO TROUBLE
WITH WINTER STORMS"*

*"CAUSES OF 'EXTREME STORM WAVES'
REMAIN A MYSTERY"*

*"VICIOUS STORM POUNDS NORTHWEST,
CLAIMING LIVES, GEAR"*

*"FEISTY SOU'EASTER TEARS UP
FISHING BOATS AND GEAR"*

Such are the headlines from issues of the *National Fisherman* magazine. Since the beginning of time, weather has ruled fishing—its friend one moment, a raging enemy the next. There is no fisherman who does not check the weather reports before going out to sea. It is one of the main reasons he carries a radio on board.

Weather, unpredictable, figures in some of the fisherman's superstitions: if a fisherman's cap blows off while he is outside on his boat, it is good luck if it blows into the water. If the cap lands on deck, however, it means there will be stormy weather.

The fisherman knows what he is up against, but that is the challenge. Weather is but one problem confronting people of the sea.

HIGHER FUEL PRICES, AND OTHER COSTS

In an industry that depends on transport, rising fuel prices have to be a main concern. In fact, more and more boat owners talk of combining motor and sail in an effort to reduce fuel costs. A skipper must go where the fish are, and he must often search the sea to find them. Fuel that once cost a fisherman running a small inshore operation on the East Coast $4,000 a year, now costs more than $10,000. And not all of that cost is covered by higher fish prices, for price per pound varies with the supply available. Smaller, older boats that are paid for may be able to absorb the higher fuel costs. Skippers on newer, larger boats, who have mortgage payments along with the fuel bills, may find it more difficult.

Besides mortgages, skippers must pay their crews, renew large insurance bills, and replace valuable gear like torn nets or broken longlines. Not too long ago, the *Cora Jean* had been night fishing in the middle of Lynn Canal, the gill net drifting nearby. During the dark hours, another boat cruised by, could not see the set, and ran through the net. It was an accident, but the expensive net had to be replaced.

RULES FOR FISHING

State and federal governments make laws so that fish have a good chance of surviving. The laws regulate the kinds of fishing gear that can be used, where and when the fishing grounds can be opened, and how many fish a boat can take during a certain period of time. Each area has a **quota**—the amount of fish that can be taken legally.

Sometimes there is a difference of opinion between the government and the fishermen. For instance, fish and game officials may say that a certain area will be open for fishing for three days. The fishermen may think that a four-day opening is a fairer amount of time. Both the fishermen and the government officials may have good reasons for their opinions. Still, the difference is there, and sometimes it causes problems.

When Rick and Dave Sorenson fish, they have rules to follow: their gill net must be only so long and so wide; the holes in the net must be a certain size; both Rick and Dave must have fishing licenses; they must fish on certain days only, for certain fish, and in certain areas; the *Cora Jean* must be licensed, too. Fishermen using other gear have regulations as well.

Such laws help preserve the fish—they are not wasted, and they are not overfished so that they disappear entirely. Neither the government officials nor the fishermen would want that.

SPREADING PROBLEMS

Some troubles may not affect the *Cora Jean* every day. On occasion, Dave Sorenson hears of oil spills or ocean dumping of wastes, and wonders what would happen to his fishing grounds with such pollutants. No one seems to know how harmful such pollution is to life under the sea. The very nature of the ocean—with its hidden depths—makes it hard to know what is going on underneath, or how one change effects another.

6

THE WORLD OF FISHING

Another day's fishing done, the *Cora Jean* tied up to the cold-storage dock in town, ready to unload. The clouds had begun to break, and patches of blue showed through. Dozens of sea gulls hoping for a fish snack circled on the air currents above.

After Rick pumped water from the hold, two cold-storage workers, almost completely covered with rubber suits, stepped down the ladder from above, onto the deck.

"How'd it go?" one of the men asked, reaching for a large bucket being lowered from above.

"Not bad for one day," Dave repled. "Ran into some rotten weather, though. Down by Bishop."

"The *Katy Jo* had trouble too," came the answer. "She took on water, but managed to get into Limestone Inlet. She's okay from last reports."

The two men jumped down into the hold and began filling the buckets with fish. When one container was full, it was hauled up onto the cold storage dock.

Above, the dock boss checked the fish over to see what condition they were in. Then he separated them according to species, filling different tubs. When the catch was up, graded, and separated, each tub was weighed. The dock boss marked down the poundage on a weight slip. Finally, he walked back to the office.

A bookkeeper, the current price list in front of her, wrote down the information on a fish-and-game ticket. Such a ticket told the government department where the fish were caught, how many were taken, and the price paid. Dave's gear card—looking like a regular credit card—showed what gear was used.

On the spot, the bookkeeper made out a check, and Dave was paid.

The *Cora Jean,* much lighter now, skimmed through the water toward the boat harbor. The sky glowed with a colorful sunset.

SHARING THE FISHERIES

The trip of the *Cora Jean* that day could have been duplicated by hundreds of boats around the world. The language of the skipper might have been different, the methods slightly changed, but the end result the same—lots of fish to sell.

Since the beginning of history, people of the world believed in freedom of the seas. That meant that ocean fish belonged to everyone, and to no one. In the water fish roam at will, fences cannot be put up, and there are no controllable boundaries. Everyone thought the sea was a magic container which never emptied of seafood. Thus, ships from different countries raced to plentiful fishing grounds and gulped up the fish—until the fish stocks became scarce.

For defense as much as fishing, nations realized they needed some sort of offshore boundary. They claimed the waters off their shores and dubbed them "territorial seas," an extension of the country. But no limit was adopted until a Dutchman, Bynkershoek, in 1703, suggested that a 3-mile (5 km) belt out from shore along a coastline belonged to that country. At that time, three miles was the range of a cannon shot—a logical distance that could be defended should an enemy or a poaching fishing ship intrude. Most nations accepted this three-mile limit, as it was a close enough area to watch and to defend.

The 1900s brought the realization that the sea was not plentiful beyond the wildest dreams, as most people thought. Fish were a renewable resource, but the fish had to be around in order to renew themselves. Humans saw the ocean stocks thin out to a dangerous degree. Judge by the near extinction of the bowhead whale and the overfishing of the yellow-fin tuna.

MAKING AGREEMENTS

To have some control over world fishing, nations drew up **treaties.** These were the rules countries set up to have a voice in what was done off their coasts. Most dealt with the crowding of vessels and gear on fishing grounds, conservation measures, and fishing "rights" which allowed one country to fish in another country's water with its permission.

Canada and the United States on both the east and west coasts have long had problems because of fishing rights. Canada, for example, might say that the fish gill-netted by the *Cora Jean* belonged to that nation, because the salmon were born in Canada. The fish were actually hatched there. Only after they were born did the reds swim through rivers to United States waters to grow. Who owns the fish then? To what country do they belong? Setting up rules will help solve such problems in a peaceful, satisfying way.

Actual steps in forming a treaty might proceed thus:

1. Representatives from each country must be sent by their governments to meet together. Perhaps they will exchange letters that say they have the authority to work on the problems.

2. Talks will continue with each side telling what it wants, and what it will give in return to solve the problems.

3. The final agreements will be printed in the language of each country and signed by the representatives.

4. The representatives take the treaty back to their own nation and have it approved by the head of the government. Other government agencies may have to approve it, too. This is called **ratification.**

5. In the final step, the representatives from the two (or more) countries again meet and exchange the approved copies of the treaty. At that time, the documents are examined carefully to be sure no changes have been made. If everything is all right, the treaty goes into force.

People of the two (or more) countries must obey these treaty rules, for then they are law. There are special rules for ending a treaty, too.

Until 1945, only the area near shore—usually limited to 3 miles (5 km)—was considered **territorial seas,** or one regulated by the adjacent country. In that year, the United Nations was established, and, with it, the new Food and Agriculture Organization (FAO), later headquartered in Rome, Italy. This agency collects world fishery figures, and directs research, among its many activities.

SAVING
THE FISHERIES

With the increased trawling of factory ships after World War II, many nations felt the need to extend their territorial waters beyond the 3-mile zone. Now most countries have extended this belt to 200 miles (322 km). That means foreign countries cannot fish in the waters 200 miles off the coast of another country without the permission of that country. The United States, too, through the Magnuson Fishery Conservation and Management Act of 1976, extended its federal limit to 200 miles. Each state may set its own internal fishery rules.

To help countries come to an understanding, international commissions such as the International North Pacific Fisheries Commission have been established. Such an organization sets quotas for catches, controls gear regulations, directs the restocking of waters for certain species, and gathers scientific information for world use, among other functions. Not every commission is successful. However, all nations want fishing to continue, so they try to set up reasonable regulations.

The *Cora Jean,* tied bow and stern to her stall in the harbor, rocked lazily on the water. The trip completed, Dave hosed the boat down, while Rick swabbed the decks with liquid soap. Soon all surfaces were clean. Then they locked the vessel and started over the floating dock for home.

The tips of the surrounding mountains caught the last of the sun's rays, and glowed a deep salmon color. The storm had left a faint salt breeze behind.

Rick took a long breath. He was tired and hungry. Yet he enjoyed fishing, and felt pleased with the day's work.

Fishing, he thought. It's a great life.

GLOSSARY

Aquaculture—the process of farming fish and shellfish in enclosed ponds or areas, where they are fed to grow faster and fatter than in their normal environment.

Autopilot—an electronic device made up of a control and a compass by which a boat is kept on a set course automatically without a person steering.

Bloom—a sudden burst of plankton growth on the ocean.

Bridge—an enclosed area on the upper part of a boat from which the ship is steered.

Coelacanth—an ancient species of fish thought to be extinct 50 million years ago, but found alive in 1938.

Continental shelf—a shelf-like table of underwater land along a coast which is no more than 100 feet (30 m) deep.

Depth finder (also called an **echo sounder**)—an electronic instrument which detects fish or obstacles by use of sound impulses which bounce off objects underwater.

Gaff—a process of hooking a fish from the water and landing it on deck. A hook with a long handle called a gaff is used.

Gill netting—a type of fishing where a net is suspended upright in the water, and the mesh opening in the net is the right size to catch certain fish by their gills.

Harpoon—a wooden or metal pole having a steel shaft with one or more barbs at the forward end to stab fish.

Hatchery—a caged-in area near water where fish eggs are hatched and where young fish are raised by people. Eventually the fish are released to open water.

Hold—a large lower compartment of a ship for the stowage of fish or cargo.

Hydraulics—a power system which helps operate machinery or other objects through the use of moving liquids such as water or oil.

Krill—an animal plankton shellfish, about two inches long, and the main food in the sea for certain whales.

Leader (gangion)—a short line with a baited hook at the end which is snapped onto the groundline at various intervals for longline fishing.

Longlining—a type of fishing where a groundline is played from a ship to lay on the sea floor or to hang suspended in the water. Anchors keep the line down and buoys show where the line is located underwater.

Magnetometer—a sensor in an autopilot unit which tells the compass when a ship is off course. The direction error is corrected automatically.

Monofilament line—a single, untwisted plastic line which is both light and strong.

Pair trawling—two boats, each with a trawl net end on board, drag the trawl bag through the water between them to catch fish.

Paralytic shellfish poisoning (PSP)—an illness resulting from eating shellfish that have been contaminated by poisonous plankton chemicals from a red tide.

Plankton—the tiny floating plants (phytoplankton) or weakly swimming animals (zooplankton) of the ocean which are the basic food for all marine life.

Puretic Power Block—a hanging block with a powered, gripping wheel which helps lift heavy fishing nets from the water onto the deck. It was developed by Mario Puretic in California during the mid-twentieth century.

Purse seining—a type of fishing where a boat, using a long net in the water, circles a school of fish, and then pulls the net bottom together, trapping the fish inside.

Quota—the number or amount for an equal share. In fishing, it would be the amount or number of fish each fisherman is allowed to catch.

Radar—an electronic device which detects nearby boats or other objects above the water's surface through the use of radio waves.

Radio direction finder (RDF)—an electronic instrument which catches a radio signal from another ship or from port, and thereby homes in on its direction.

Ratification—the process of two or more countries legally and formally approving something, such as a treaty.

Red tide—a patchy condition on the ocean from a tremendous flowering of plankton plants and animals.

Salinity—consisting of or relating to salt, as the amount of salt in ocean water.

Scoop net—a large or small net shaped like a bowl with rigid material circling the top. The net is on a long pole and is handled by one person to scoop fish from the water.

Shellfish dredging—a type of fishing where one or more metal arms are extended from a boat into the water. At the sea end of the arm is attached a large, strong bag on an iron frame which is dragged over the bottom, collecting shellfish.

Skates—a section of a longline which lays along the bottom, consisting of lines and hooks, and with buoys and anchors at either end. Many skates can be fastened together to make a longer groundline.

Spear—a long stick or rod with one or more points at the end. Ropes are attached to some spears so that they, and the fish, can be retrieved.

Starboard—looking forward on a vessel, starboard is the right side. The left side is called the port side.

Territorial seas—a belt of water and underwater land along the coast of a country, the ownership of which belongs to that nation.

Tong—a long shaft with clasping grips at the end. These are used primarily to pick up shellfish from the bottom.

Trammel net—a triple wall of netting suspended upright in the water. Fish swim through the larger outer netting from either side, and into the central net where they are entangled.

Trawling—a method of fishing by which a ship pulls a net bag through the water.

Treaty—a formal, written, and signed agreement between two or more countries.

Trolling—a type of fishing where baited hooks on lines are trailed through the water from a moving boat.

Weir trap—a type of fishing trap in which walls of netting, suspended from floats or framing, are constructed in such a way as to guide fish through a tunnel of netting into the "heart" of the trap where they cannot find their way out. Some such traps have a bottom of netting as well.

Zooplankton—a tiny animal plankton which swims weakly in ocean water, and is a primary food for many marine creatures.

SUGGESTIONS FOR FURTHER READING

Arnow, Boris, Jr. *Homes Beneath the Sea.* Boston: Little, Brown, 1969.

Asimov, Isaac. *How Did We Find Out About Life in the Deep Sea?* New York: Walker, 1982.

Dugan, James. *Underwater Explorer: The Story of Captain Cousteau.* New York: Harper and Row, 1957.

Meltzer, Michael. *The World of the Small Commercial Fishermen.* New York: Dover, 1980.

Rahn, Joan Elma. *Traps and Lures in the Living World.* New York: Atheneum, 1980.

Shannon, Terry, and Payzan, Charles T. *Windows in the Sea: New Vehicles That Scan the Ocean Depths.* Chicago: Children's Press, 1973.

Sturges, Patricia Patterson. *The Endless Chain of Nature.* Philadelphia: Westminster, 1976.

Swenson, Allen A. *The World Within the Tidal Pool.* New York: McKay, 1979.

Tunis, Edwin. *Oars, Sails and Steam: A Picture Book of Ships.* New York: T. Y. Crowell, 1952.

For further information in the United States and Canada, write to the following:

Food and Agricultural
Organization
Public Information Office
United Nations
1776 F Street, NW
Washington, DC 20437

Fisheries and Oceans
Government of Canada

Main Offices
240 Sparks Street
Ottawa, Canada K1A OE6

Pacific Region
1090 West Pender Street
Vancouver, BC Canada
V6E 2P1

International North Pacific
Fisheries Commission
6640 NW Marine Drive
Vancouver, BC, Canada V6T 1X2

National Oceanic and
Atmospheric Administration
National Marine Fisheries Service
U.S. Department of Commerce
Washington, DC 20235

INDEX